BONES OF A VERY FINE HAND

MARJORIE SAISER

THE BACKWATERS PRESS
OMAHA

Acknowledgements:

Some of the poems in this volume have appeared, some in slightly different versions, in: *Georgia Review, Prairie Schooner, The Denny Poems, Zone 3, Cumberland Poetry Review, Cimarron Review, Sow's Ear Review, Yarrow, Cream City Review, Whole Notes, Laurel Review, Madison Review, Crazy Horse*, and in *Leaning into the Wind*, an anthology from Houghton-Mifflin.

Photo of the poet by Hilda Raz, Copyright © 1999.

Cover Art "Downy Gentian, Grasshopper", Wendy Jane Bantam, Copyright © 1999, oil on canvas, 15"x11".

All poems copyright © Marjorie Saiser, 1999

Backwaters Press logo designed by L.L. Mannlein. Copyright © 1997 Backwaters Press.

First printing, 750 copies, June, 1999.

Published by: The Backwaters Press
                  Greg Kosmicki, Editor/Publisher
                  3502 North 52nd Street
                  Omaha, Nebraska 68104-3506
                  (402) 451-4052
                  GKosm62735@aol.com

ISBN: 0-7392-0284-7

Library of Congress Catalog Card Number: 99-95251

Printed in theUnited States of America by
Morris Publishing Co • 3212 E Hwy 30 • Kearney, NE 68847

Marjorie Saiser

Bones of a Very Fine Hand

Many thanks to these supporters of The Backwaters Press,
without whose generous contributions and subscriptions
the publication of this book would not have been possible:

ANGELS

Steve and Kathy Kloch
Rich and Eileen Zochol

BENEFACTORS

Barbara Schmitz

PATRONS

Maureen Toberer
Frederick Zydek

SPONSORS

Paul and Mildred Kosmicki
Gary Leisman and Wendy Adams
Jeff and Patti Knag
Matt Mason
Pat Murray and Jeanne Schuler
Anne Potter
Carol Schmid
Alan and Kim Stoler
Don Taylor

FRIENDS

J.V. Brummels
Twyla Hansen
Tim O'Connor
Jim and Mary Pipher
Richard White

for my mother

for Don, Paul, Sue

Bones of a Very Fine Hand

Anna in the Swing

While the Mind Is Clear 1
Once 3
Killing Snakes 4
I See Her Hand 5
The Green Coat 6
I Want This Picture 7
She Killed Crickets in the House 8
She Heard No Laughter 9
Potato Soup 11
I Want to Create 13
Anna in the Swing 15
Making Noodles 18
I Am Not at Home 19
Going to See the Home Place 20
There Is the Rain 21

I Tell Her of the Downy Gentian

We Get the News 25
My Daughter, Afraid 27
Seeing the Baby 29
Washing the Walls 30
Cutting My Hair 32
I Was Not There 33
My Daughter Asks if I Was Happy 34
I Tell Her Stories 36
I Let My Daughter Down 37
Shopping 38
Loving Her in the Mountains 39
I Tell Her of the Downy Gentian 40
Looking for Luck 41
Last Sunday 42
Naming 43
How is Paul? 45
Looking for Meteors 47
Assateague Island, October 48

Practically One

In the Pacific 53
Letter from My Father 54
Practically One 55
On the Bridge, Spring Thaw 56
The Dahlias My Mother Gave Me 57
Letter to My Daughter 58
The Wind Picks Up 59
He Rang the Bell 61
I Broke My Mother's Dish 63
I Don't Want to Think about You 64
Pulling Up Beside My Husband at the Stoplight 66
I Hear You in the Morning 67
I Lie About My Life 69
Getting Well in the Mountains 70
Taking the Baby to the Marsh 72
She Asks for Baby Pictures 73

In the Rain

Resurrection 77
When I Sliced through the Nail 78
White Semi 79
Asking 81
It's Been Written 82
Becoming My Father 84
Wind Tore at Her House 85
Why We Last 86
Perfume Counter, Dillards 87
Saying Yes on the Road 88
Afraid to Be Old 89
Why Do You Remember Your Father's Suit 90
The Last Thing He Said 92
The World Was Not Enough 93
Saving the Photograph 94
My Son Cooks 95
When She Calls 97
In the Rain 98
My Old Aunts Play Canasta in a Snowstorm 99
Keeping My Mother Warm 100
Storm at Night 101
Having this Afternoon Turned Away 102

As If I Were Looking at Photographs   104
Today   105

Foreword

KEEPING ON

> I want to create, bring forth,
> to say, *Let there be.*

Marge Saiser's first book-length collection of poems is an act of creation that reflects the poet's distinctive vision and equally distinctive imagination. Near the end of the book, for example, she ruefully anticipates growing old, "to have someone paid / to place food into your mouth," while early in the book her imagination permits her to see her mother "turning eggs on a wire shelf in the incubator," to see her father as "a plains boy in New Guinea / carrying among the baby pictures my / mother young and true and lovely, / long legs bared to the sun," to perceive her grandmother as artist: "What if she'd sketched / every day after the dishes? The fire burning, / the coal and not the woman whispering, / the sound of pencil touching paper."

Neither her vision nor her imagination glosses those persistent sadnesses--divorce, illness, old age, death--but neither do they deny those joyful epiphanies that can sometimes serve to counterbalance misery. Anticipating the birth of her first grandchild, Saiser writes, "This beloved bird that tapped daily / on the wall of your body will lie // in the crook of your arm." Here, she is speaking to her daughter. In other poems she will speak to and about her son, her husband, her grandmother, her aunts and uncles, herself-- sometimes revealing herself in first person, at other times presenting herself in the guise of Anna.

Both Anna and Marge Saiser appreciate that the whole truth, and nothing but, is probably impossible to come by. When the poet says, "I lie about my life," she is probably very much aware of the significant distinction between fact and truth. She knows a hawk from a handsaw. If some of her details are invented (and I doubt that many of them are), they serve to underscore honest and fundamental perceptions--and therein lie the "truths." Here is one of them, the desire for solitude--the final five lines of "I Was Not There":

> Sometimes I want to be alone in the cabin, a room
> by myself when the moon shines in. I want
> the others to go ahead on the trail.
> I walk alone then,
> laying my hand on the bark of the trees.

At other times she prefers the company of others, family especially, and while she is with them, through rough times and smooth, she sees herself as part of a community much larger than immediate family. In "Storm at Night," for example, she lies awake early in the morning on Indian Island, thinking of friends, thinking of Crazy Horse "who / before he died, asked for the man who had / pushed the bayonet into the soft parts of his back," thinking of her daughter, thinking of the nearby Platte "wrinkling over its sand bars, / around the smooth white bones / of its cottonwood logs."

These poems are filled with specifics that lead finally to measured affirmation. Pebbles, chickweed, barn and house and bread, cookstove and clock, cream and quilt, pillow and bedsheet, pasture and crowbar, hollyhock, mason jar, workboots and teakettle and arrowroot cookies, bullsnake, cucumber vine, redbud and forsythia: "This apple, this Macintosh, this knife...." The eye sees. The ear hears. All of the senses are aroused, and collectively they dramatize the truths and the half-truths of human existence. "The whole world has happened before," Saiser writes, but that doesn't mean that either the world or the writing is finished. "I'm writing it / all again," she says, "words once again / one after another, // as a pebble puts down its rings, / as many as it can / on its way to the bottom...."

It arrives at last in guarded affirmation. Anna, in her swing, looks beyond a barbwire fence to see a red horse, "a stud cropping grass, / sound of his teeth tearing stems, his tail / switching at flies on his haunches, his / black sex hanging down, / telling the truth, lying." Lying *and* telling the truth? Lying *by* telling the truth? Both? Later, in "When She Calls," Saiser writes of her grandmother and her own daughter, both "blindsided by blackness / on any given morning"; even so, each in her own way, the poet says, turns "back to the house or the barn, / to the field or the table, keeping on / keeping on."

In a voice both fresh and accessible these poems reflect an enduring persistence; eventually the light turns green, "and there's another song coming." Add to this the poet's wry sense of humor, a pleasant and puckish attitude that might well make the business of "keeping on" possible. There are many bones in this book, and many fine hands. Saiser's willingness occasionally to chuckle at and with them (her own included) leads to a healthy, though difficult, affirmation. Her poems, having cleared their throats, sing; they make connections that, for better or worse, through sickness and health, provide the ties that keep right on binding.

--William Kloefkorn

Lincoln, Nebraska, 1999

Anna In The Swing

While the Mind Is Clear

My mother sorts her photographs
at the kitchen table, a pile for
each daughter. She pauses,
picture in hand: women
in front of a car, someone's foot
on the running board, ankle
and heel and new leather,
the cock of elbows. This
is what she has, indelible.

What I have: the long afternoon at the cabin
when my daughter and I killed the mosquitoes,
kept them from the baby's neck and ears,
caught them in our hands,

her hand or my hand closing on them.
Big mosquitoes, these lake mosquitoes,
my daughter said. *Big but slow.*
We flattened them against the wall,
or let them land on the forearm
where we smeared them harmless,

the child sleeping, the cabin quiet,
long shade of trees around us, blue
of the lake in the window.
This remains: the long afternoon,
the cardinal on the boards of the deck,
cat coming to the door.
This remains: we worked, wordless,
signed to each other

where the enemy was and who should strike.
The baby slept, breath and breath and breath.
We read or napped, the loaf uncut
on the table, the pie three-quarters gone,
the simple rice, boys with fishing poles
passing our cabin on the way to the pier.
Faded formica of the tabletop, slow whir
of fans, stacks of books.
As long as the mind is clear:

moments alone at the water's edge. My mother
sorts her photographs, thinks who should
have this one or that one. I watch her hands
choosing and lifting and turning a photograph,
my mother alone with some moment she had,
and has, and will lose. My daughter
and I, the pair of us, moving in the cabin
against mosquitoes, breeze filling the curtain.
My mother does not speak,
the ends of her fingers holding
some black and white morning or afternoon,
light and shade over the grass or
over the sand, the screen house empty,
the red-eyed loons diving
out of sight into the lake.

Once

Under a clothesline she stood
almost as if dancing:
self-conscious, proud, happy
in sunshine in a backyard I've never seen,
before a camera I've only imagined
in the hands of a man who was my
father. I was in the house

or in the shade in a wicker buggy
by the back door, sleeping or looking up
at the curve of perambulator sky,
my father taking my mother's picture,
loving the length of her legs and
her daring, coming into sunshine
to have her picture taken: dark hair,
two-piece sunsuit, ties hanging
in the middle of the pale skin
of her stomach, sunsuit always
green print to my eye after the one
brief time I saw the black and white
photo. As surely as it was green,
it was indeed purchased
on the base or maybe at Woolworth's
in downtown El Paso. He wanted her to

wear it, that's the truth as surely
as the click of a shutter, black square-
cornered box held squarely in his hands,
in his hands the small photograph he would
place into the billfold he would
push down into his back pocket.
Duffle bag, bus, troop carrier,
up the walkway, looking back once,
crossing the equator, a plains boy in New Guinea
carrying among the baby pictures my
mother young and true and lovely,
long legs bared to the sun.

Killing Snakes

The head of the snake backs away
from my mother, backs away
above its body, its body in coils
against the row of onions,
its tail shaking out a noise;
my mother's arms, her hoe
raised above her head.
Down like a judgment. The head of the snake is
tail-less before her, its jaws opening and closing,
its body a whip in the radish leaves,
whipping slower, whipping
looser. She holds the handle
of the hoe, resting the blade
on the ground, studies

the cards that have been played,
playing her own cards close to her vest,
conversation flowing by around her.
She sees a way, if she can get rid of
three losers, just three, just two,
just this one more trick past
that unsuspecting Vera who is so
intent on getting no hearts.

Ah, the jack. That does it. My mother brings
down swiftly the ten, king, queen, and ace.
All you holding cards around this table:
what you are dealing with
none of you can know,
not one of you has any idea.

I See Her Hand

I see her hand coming across the table toward me
to lay her card, most likely the jack,
into the center; she is telling her stories, turning
sentences carefully. I think of her, a child
turning eggs on a wire shelf in the incubator,
the chicks curled in the shells.
She watched the fire, kept it going,
the chicks nothing but spots on the yolks,
sprouting wings, crowding their spaces.
Twenty-one days keeping the fire,
her grandmother's brief important instructions:
not too hot, for that would kill the chicks,

no second chances. Not too low
or the chicks would jell and cease.
The red line of the thermometer hovering
like a breath at the right place,
twenty-one days the charcoal carefully
laid on time into the pile, the eggs
moved on time from the edges to the center.
Across from me at the table she is happy,

or she is angry at some injustice,
an old wrong smoldering. It is her job to care
for what is yet to come; she turns the eggs,
the smell of the brooder house around her,
the sound a slow collapsing into ash.
Her first charge not yet pipping,
not yet the important triangular opening.
Faithful to her task, her watch,
the last time for the night,
the early time in the dawn,
taking off her mitten, her hand
on the warm shell, close to the pulse,
fingering a curve of wall I sleep against.

The Green Coat

It was a good wool and a good cut,
gold-colored buttons heavy and embossed;
shawl collar lying on her straight shoulders.
She came out of the living quarters into
the kitchen in the green coat,

no one in the cafe but her brother
at the counter and her husband talking
to him, these two men having bought
the coat in Spencer, having brought it to her.
They had been waiting and she coughed
in the way she did when she didn't

know what to say. She unbuttoned
the button, slid her hand into the pocket.
Her husband came into the kitchen,
giving a wolf-whistle. Her hair brushed back,
a woman with good bones, long legs
and Irish-English hands, her lashes
on her cheeks, her eyes looking at the floor.

I Want This Picture

I want this picture of my grandmother
this picture in the locket:
Ruby sitting on the sofa in the yard
the yard blown nearly clean of chicken feathers
columns of the porch behind her,
her thick ankles crossed,
new shoes on,
her back straight.
Someone carried the couch
out to the yard for the picture.
Maybe she helped with that herself.
I want to think she did.
And beside her in the locket
the other:
her sweetheart on a horse
his hat on the back of his head
the sun on his face
his eyes looking out of the photograph
straight into the eyes of Ruby,
of me.
His horse wanting to escape from picture-taking
but easy for a man of his size to manage;
a man big enough to give this locket,
to buy it on main street
and to write her a postcard
about Sunday night
so she'd be ready
and I think she was
her hair waved
the locket arranged
against the bosom of her blue dress.
I want this picture, Ruby,
before the silences walked with you
the farm gone,
the twins crying, pulling at your skirt.
I want this picture:
this man, this woman,
all of us,
about to bolt toward something promising.

She Killed Crickets in the House

On her hands and knees behind the washtubs,
only her broken black shoes
and her brown cotton legs showing,
she searched out the chirping
and subdued it.

After that the cosmos
on the south side
did not do well,
the dill dried up,
the hens grayed, the canary
choked and died,
the old man put three sheep
into the houseyard.

Her jaw squared as she
watched from the window.
The sheep ate the young fruit trees.
Useless the rolls of chicken wire
she struggled to bring them.

Unprotected her round heavy body
walking home from town Wednesday nights,
the eye of her flashlight
washing back and forth on the gravel,
the stark white ragweeds.

She Heard No Laughter

She heard no laughter most
days, did not have conversation, and so
she took up talking to herself, whispering
what she was thinking, mostly
about her husband, the sourness of her life
deposited daily in him. What if she had been

jolly? What if she'd set to work to draw?
Filling a notebook with pictures of the old
stove, the window, the holes in the lace
of the curtain, the shape of the door in the
canary's cage. What if she'd sketched
every day after the dishes? The fire burning,
the coal and not the woman whispering,
the sound of pencil touching paper.
What if she'd drawn the cedar tree? The pencil
catching the way the boughs lay down the wind
when they are through with it. What if she'd drawn
stick cats and birds and rabbits with loopy ears,

drawn these things for her granddaughter?
Drawn the fine loaves baking, shading
them as well as placing them on their
sides on the tea towel. What if she'd
sketched her granddaughter's face?
What if she'd tried for the hair, the cowlick?
And told the child stories, one each day.
The child in her lap, the rocker
creaking the long afternoon,
saying some days *Chi-ca-go, Chi-ca-go,*
some days saying *Ant-arc-tica, Ant-arc-tica.*
The rocker and the canary and the pictures.

Sketching in winter the memory of
the flower garden, the cosmos by the door
falling over, the dill strong and brown
through the fall, the tender throat of
snapdragon. What if she'd drawn the sleeping
child? The drop of sweat, the measles, wet
hair over the forehead. Sun and shade on the floor
different every day. What if she'd

been happy? What if I pretend she was?
Any day out the south window
imaginary guinea fowl strutting the yard.
A fence around the house. A red
barn, black and white cows loafing, white
bags of breath above their noses. Hogs
rooting the feeders, banging the lids.
Her son, her dead son, alive and well

carrying a pail down to the barn,
double thumbs of his chore mittens,
earflaps up, jaunty in his denim jacket,
jaunty in his eight-buckle overshoes.
Her house full of books, white
plates, silver spoons, forks nesting
against themselves in red velvet
drawers of the china cabinet. In the cellar,
applesauce like nectar in the jars.

Potato Soup

put one foot on a chair
turn the peelings in long ribbons
into the metal pan on the table

not quite under your breath curse him

say he is pigheaded and tight
say he should not expect it say
nowhere in the gold locket
opening to the strong dark

face did it promise
you would run down bugs in a house not
fit for the goat woman

nowhere in the new grass the crickets
the stars did it prophesy coal dust

say your mother warned you
against Irish against strong fingers

chop them into convenient sizes
the potatoes
the onions
she warned he would smell of onions

while it is boiling throw
the peelings to the chickens
wipe your hand on your coat
not even a decent henhouse

milk and butter and salt
float the pepper on the top
turn the gas low at least it's
not cobs

slice an apple for the canary
it hasn't sung for days

rock

the squeak of the wood comforts as
the light goes down
and down

on the east wall the everyday
pattern of lace and cedar branches
fading

rise

stir

the children are gone except Davy
Charles is dead under this snow

when he opens the door tell him
it is ready

I Want to Create

I want to create, bring forth,
to say *Let there be.* To make a heron
rise off the pond, tucking his neck
into the shape I want to give it,
flapping his wings enough to clear
the cedars, to clear me,
watching as I am at the fence
in the sunflowers. I want to
create my grandmother looking
in the ragweed for the money I dropped.
I want her to search and search for it,
nickels and dimes and pennies

in the knot in the corner of
the lavender hanky, to look for it
at the base of the ragweed stems
as if she were searching for me,
as if she could find what is lost,
what is missing. I want to watch,
her back rounded, bent over,
the buttons of the thin summer
housedress, her stockings
in the hot sun, her hair coming
out of the roll, looking for what
cannot be found. I want someone
to believe the heron, believe the need
for the loaf of bread, believe the spine,
the woman bending over, to believe

the coins, missing, to believe she forgave me,
came out to the overgrown field and looked
for it, the impossible loss, the sun
beating down on us, the shade of blue
over the wings and the back, the lift-off
from a prairie pond. I want someone
to believe the pond, the air over the pond,
the flapping of wings as of a manta's
arms over the floor of the ocean. I want
someone--I want to be the one--to stand up,
to hold the lost--

                    rediscovered and powerful

in the palm of the hand, to say with
amazement: *Look, I found it.*

Anna in the Swing

I sat in the classroom, my arms folded,
my feet crossed in front of me while
the professor talked on about point of view.
I sat up and began to write a story, writing
twelve-year-old Anna in the
wooden swing in the big tree,
the swing rising in its arc
over the fence, back into the yard,
back out over the fence, where two
young hogs were copulating in
oak leaves, or trying to,
their rounded white backs humping,
Anna in the swing watching them,
the jays screaming *stop, stop* in the
shade inside the oak tree above her head,
Uncle Michael behind the screen door
watching Anna watching the hogs.

In the story, I called Uncle Michael
Rheinhold, and I called myself
Anna, a soft and yielding name.
All the while I was writing the swing
and the jays and Michael/Rheinhold, I
was answering some of the professor's
questions, an old part of me replying,
measuring, generalizing, and

a new part of me in the swing, writing
fast on the paper because the story was
clear but fragile as a small pile of
leaves in wind. I left the room
when the others left, and I sat
on a stone bench near the library. Anna
sat on the slatted seat looking over her
shoulder, looking over the fence,
her tanned arm lying on the
back of the swing. The fence looming,
falling back. The swing rising
toward the white farmhouse,
. her appleprint dress
fluttering as she traveled

again out over the fence,
I on my bench hearing and
writing the scream of the jays
and the sound of the swing ropes rubbing
into the limb of the oak, seeing

the white-haired grandmother small and
thin, her back rounded like a bolster,
her shoes softly ticking on the linoleum,
her hands carrying a jar of cream to the table,
or lifting a plate of kuchen,
a pinwheel of apple slices on top.
The voice of the grandmother
in the dark in the bed beside the sleepless
Anna. Anna staring at the window:
rectangle defined by moonlight and breeze.
The drone of cicadas, rising, falling.

The next morning in clear light I wanted to
write down the smell of the haymow, the fear
and pleasure of the ladder, the heavy bones
and black and white hides of the cows below
in the stanchions, the uncle milking, the
cats waiting. I wanted words for them,
places. Swinging out and back,
the farmyard, the wilderness,
the truth, the lie. An outdoor

shower near the pine grove, water
in the shallow tank in the top of it,
warmed all day by the sun but not
overwarm on the skin and the scalp,
not enough for luxury. Real, unreal,
smell of soap and pine trees.
A red wound on Anna's shin where
her leg slid between bales in the loft,
the water and soap stinging the scrape.
Rheinhold's eyes and his words,

murmuring. Anna on the hillside
watching a red horse across a barbwire
fence, a stud cropping grass,
sound of his teeth tearing stems, his tail
switching at flies on his haunches, his
black sex hanging down,
telling the truth, lying.

Making Noodles

Choose the music; play it loud for yourself
and your house on a Sunday morning.
Watch a finch at the feeder, watch

the pen and ink of her wingbars.
She looks at the sky, the ground.
Her head and shoulders
moving: lights turning on.
The feeder sways with her,
chaff drifting in the wind.
Break the egg. Beat the milk,
salt, flour. Roll the noodles

without fuss, a sureness in your
hands as if from some grandmother,
a grandmother you've not seen:
cotton scarf around her head,
her hands like yours taking flour
in the creases of skin,
around the nails, inside the rings.
Her hair, if not for the scarf,

surely hanging and swaying
around her face. Sing,
cut the noodles,
lay them on the cloth.

Praise the father. Praise the mother.
The finch who faces into the wind,
who finds her seeds.

Your grandmother's fingers,
your grandmother's hands, your song
going out to the house, to the chairs and rugs,
to the walls, the pictures,
beyond the windows,
beyond the frost on the grass,
beyond.

I Am Not at Home

I am not at home in my hometown.
One night I pull what I know about it
around the streets and houses,
a wagon dragged by a dog in harness,
my old boxer Freddie going where he wants.
I walk beside his head,

bumping his thick brown neck to turn him.
Not at home in the raised iron letters on the town pump,
in the gravel of the road, the pebbles, chickweed,
oilspots on the ground at the filling station.
The mayor burns trash in the street

next to the long clapboard of his grocery store,
burns an old grapefruit he couldn't sell,
and a few newspapers. If he were
to call hello to me, his white breath rising
from the ring of his mouth,
I would stand under the streetlight,
mute refugee
in a circle of pale cold light.

Going to See the Home Place

We climb into the pickup, going to see the home place,
although, my father says, there's nothing left.

Two miles south of town I open the gate.
A calf watches,
her black and white face
new and stark, all the edges undefiled.

Until things changed, my father says,
the house was there, west of the trees.
The barn, it was beautiful,
red and white stripes
on the cupola. The spring,

cold water day and night
flowing into the barrel,
spilling over the top.

Almost at the gate I remember
to ask where the strawberries were.
I find the clump of trees
at the end of my father's pointing finger.
Not the first draw, but the second.
Strawberries, he says, carried out by the dishpanful.

The home place at the far reaches of his finger
goes down to the river
goes north to Julius's
goes high and pretty
between the bluffs and the trees,
rolls with his hand

blows with the wind:
I myself am seeing it, taking
the measure of it with my arms,
as if his grandmother,
with my uncalloused hands,
unfurled a farm
like a sheet
into morning air.

There Is the Rain

There is the rain, the woman,
young, pregnant, the contractions
starting, the pain she is afraid of,
rain on the small house where she lies,
rain in the morning in that
country of corn rows,
of doves on the telephone wires
and mallards in the water
along the side of the road,
light coming from gray clouds

into the window, her parents
sleeping in the next room. Soon
she will have to wake her father
to take her to the hospital. She
has had no luxury except one:
a bond she cashed to order
a layette from the catalog,
the small white shirts
and pastel sleepers. She
salvaged a crib, found

a way, has sewn for him,
thin patterns laid on the cotton,
placed with her fingers,
cut with her new scissors,
the child resting in her belly
as if in her lap. This morning
cold rain taps its nails
against the north window.
She thinks someday the child
will ask for help. She will say
yes, I'll come, yes, I'll keep you safe,
yes, anything, yes.

I Tell Her Of The Downy Gentian

We Get the News

Tonight I drive in the northern part of the county,
the clouds dark as a bruise, rain beating in the headlights,
thunder folding and unfolding.

Last night my daughter called with the news:
she's pregnant. My husband in his pajamas
held the receiver to his ear; I sat on the floor
with the other phone to hear the news.

My grandchild: a syncopated rhythm
pummeling as if with small hooves my daughter's belly.

My husband and I lay in the dark,
trying to sleep, the news ricocheting from wall to wall
in the quiet bedroom. I got up to write *Dear Baby*
in my notebook. *Dear Baby, Welcome.*

In a city on the coast my son knows none of this news,
not yet knowing of his sister's child, thinking forward
perhaps to business in the morning,
the important motions and statutes and arguments,
shucking at last tonight his business clothes and shoes,
wearing perhaps a towel, his feet bare,
sitting in front of the TV or his papers
or books, knowing the details of
the upcoming case but not knowing
his sister's list of names for the baby.

Flower in my daughter's narrow body,
I want to think there is that which prevails.

My son watches the screen. There are
car bombs, there is debris,
there are flags, and faces shouting.

Lightning bleaches the street and the trees.
On the windshield just now a pattern

of water like craters on a moon map.

Dear Baby

In a medium-sized midwestern city
in the northern part of a county
there is the good smell of rain,
the sweet slap of the drops against my arm
and into my outstretched hand.

You are loved.

My Daughter, Afraid

What can I tell her?

That everything will be all right?
That there is nothing scary or bad, out of our control,
that there is a god whose eye is on the sparrow?
My daughter is afraid because of numbers
on a blood test. Because she is afraid,

because I am afraid, I tell her how it will be:
the baby, born smiling and speaking couplets,
will be a ham, I say. I say, the baby will crack
a bad joke for the doctor. You, supine, will
applaud. The cord will be cut and you will be
reunited. This beloved bird that tapped daily
on the wall of your body will lie

in the crook of your arm.
In this version we hold the child
on a porch at a cabin on a lake
in the mornings and the evenings. We teach
her how to say *loon*, how to say *eagle*. In this version
there is no spina bifida, no syndrome, no Rh

negative. Everything unkind lies soft on the bottom
of the lake, being gummed by--about to become
scales and fin of--that good slow-moving
large-mouthed god, carp. In this version
there is no fear, no young woman crying.
In this version there are flight feathers for each eagle,
rising, gathering. In this version the eye of the bird

can see clearly each toe and finger
of the child on the lap of the woman on the porch,
the fin of each foolish perch, each circling bass.
In this version the loon, that ancient
which cannot walk on land,
swims safely on the lake, safely dives and surfaces,
treads over the safest deepest water. In this version
the child, eagle-eyed, watches the white plate

of the moon above the black house of the pines.
In this version I can see the child's hand,
the fingers spread in mid-
air, her face and body alive, safe,
listening,
her eye in the dark
bright with the will to hear it:
my daughter laughing, I laughing,
the cry of the loon.

Seeing the Baby

In the ultrasound pictures
his bonewhite face shows
the hollows which are his eyes,
sleeping or blinking in the dark,
the bones white on black
in the scratchy floppy pictures
in my daughter's hand,
my daughter wanting to show him
wanting to see him
her hand now and then on her belly
her fingers tracing on the pictures
smeared images of bone,
making me see her son.
She shows me;
            I see you,
your face a thousand years old,
a mummy, eyeless, hairless,
caught perhaps in the middle of a yawn.
She is excited over the jingle bells,
your genitals hanging heavy
between the bones of your legs.
If you were female, you'd
have your eggs in sacs, ready,
though you wouldn't need them for years.
This sac you have now
hanging in water.
Her fingernail taps the line between

the halves of your brain.
Here the bottom of your foot against the womb.
She shows me your toes
your fingers, the bones of your arms,
your fists on either side of your white face.
I say to you, Bones,
Egyptian,
not listening,

mummy my daughter loves
I say:

Me, too.
Me, too.

Washing the Walls

My daughter wants the house clean, wants me to
leave my shoes at the door. She's nesting,
large and tired, awaiting the child. This is a way

I love her: I'm on a ladder
washing the walls, washing windows,
my hand over the ledges and sills
and floors of her house,
my hand across glass
corner to corner to corner.

Tonight she rests in a chair and reads to me
comics and editorials while I dust the blinds.
I laugh and I clean. Another joke, another slat.
We talk about the time I was pregnant with her.
She wants to know these things,
how she fits in, how her child fits in;
she is fierce to prepare the bed
and the clothes for him,
the books and music. Now she sits
crosslegged before her shelves
and shows me what she has,
what is ready. Once before sunrise

she pulled her luggage down the streets
of Oxford to the Greenline busstop.
After cold cereal at the landlady's,
the sound of the wheels of her suitcase
on the sidewalk to the bus and then the plane.
All that day in my mind
I watched the winter storms, her path unlit
until it opened like a fallopian tube to a place
where I waited to gather her, safe and home,

waited as now she waits. She touches her belly,
her fingers circling, keeping the searchlight on,
sweeping the dark. It's her child. Nobody

will love him as she does, watching his progress
over the pole, the strong winds at the higher
elevations, the crackpots in the airports
with guns and explosives and axes to grind,
nobody assigned to the child as she is assigned.

My gift: these moist surfaces,
the shine of the wood,
the peppermint soap in the rag,
my hand moving

along the baseboards,
drawing boundaries,
my hand washing the walls,
this for the love of her

who lay in the dark of my body
as now, still, the thought of her
lies light and steady where
hope is, where it stays, where it lives.

Cutting My Hair

Heavy with the child, my daughter
kneels behind my chair on newspapers
spread on her kitchen floor. She's
cutting my hair; I'm crying and

mad because I'm making things worse
by crying. I want to stop this haircut.
Half-done is fine with me. I grab her
wrist behind my head, but she pulls away.
We struggle: a pregnant woman on her knees,
and her mother, holding her wrist.
I'm just as stubborn, she says,

and more so. She won't stop cutting
and cutting. I sit with my face in the
towel. She says *It's all right,*
forget it, let me finish
this, let me do what I have to do.
I let her cut my hair, small pieces falling,
shedding onto the flannel shirt
she wears over the baby. Near my ear

the hairs grate against the blade,
steady, slow. Her knees shift
the papers as she circles me.
It's guilt, she says. *I've had it too,*
I've had it plenty.
My face in the towel,
my head at the angle for the haircut,
I can't stop her cutting,

parting, combing,
making me feel better.
When I finish here, she says,
you'll be ready for a hug.

I Was Not There

I was not there when my daughter gave birth,
when before the last push, the doctor asked
Do you want to feel your baby's head?
She guided my daughter's hand down
to touch the child about to be born,
a first blessing from his mother.
It is a story my daughter tells me.
I would have been there; I'd heard
of a grandmother who asked, as she
caught the child in her arms, Where

did you come from, tell me before you forget.
The story my daughter tells me is her body
groaning and parting, long and full of pain.
In the story she knew her son before she saw him,
the vernix over his eyelids, over his cheeks.
She knew his cry. She says she needed to
do this by herself, for the new family.

Sometimes I want to be alone in the cabin, a room
by myself when the moon shines in. I want
the others to go ahead on the trail.
I walk alone then,
laying my hand on the bark of the trees.

My Daughter Asks if I Was Happy

She wants to know how it was,
divorce, things not turning out.
I tell her I was completely
oblivious. It's as good as being brave,
I say. She is watching me with her baby,

his arms flashing out, his hand
pulling the hair near my ear. My daughter
is surprised that I was happy.
I can remember the day it began, I say--
I can remember the minute.
I was rolling in the grass with you, I tell her,

in May in the yard at that place on
Fremont Street; I remember the brown
western shirt I was wearing and the jeans.
I laughed and rolled in the grass, tumbling
my daughter around, and I had things to be
doing in the house, but I stayed outside,
my husband not coming home, coming home
late again and going out a lot, and you, the child
in my arms, asked me, Why don't you
always stay like this, playing with us, I like you like this.

I remember the shift, the turning,
the grass and the plowed garden plot
and the alley, and the neighbors to the east
behind the row of trees, and there in that sun-on-
poplars time, a wind twirling small round leaves,
I began.

I try to tell her how it was, that turning
in the sun and the shade, the wheelbarrow
and the unfinished patio. I can't tell her

of course, but she seems to want
to try to get it
and I want her to have it,
that green and gold moment.
I tell her: When you asked me
I said Yes.
Yes.

I Tell Her Stories

It seems necessary to tell my daughter
about that time she burned her hand at the babysitter's,
and what I fed her during her first winter:
whatever Gerber had in babyfood jars.
I mashed a ripe banana or gave little pieces

of buttered bread. I tell about the white Ford
my father gave me, the way it purred, the fact
that it had a plastic bucket upside down
for the passenger seat. I tell how I laughed
when she took the neighbor child's doll,
carried it into the bathroom to take off
the clothes and the head,
her face intent when I found her,
how funny and wonderful she looked,

working hard. How calm I was when
she cut her chin, falling in the bathtub, how I
carried her, wet in a towel, didn't want to
frighten her, how the men at the emergency room
sewed her skin and I held her baby hands. Please, I want to say,
is it OK? I shut off
the car; we sit in the drive and I keep telling.
I've got to know.

I Let My Daughter Down

She brings home a cardboard box,
opens the lid, her hands sleek,
moving as if ready to weave
or play a stringed instrument.
She lifts out a chick and gives it
to me. Nobody, she says,
would take this one.

The feet of the chick are
wads of toes. He sits on his
elbows. Something happened,
I say, in the egg. My daughter's eyes
are lovely. Fairness. A chance
for everybody. She names him
Pegasus.

We set his box in the basement
bathroom away from the cats.
The dandelion fuzz on Pegasus
goes to pinfeathers. He straddles
bravely, the distance from one
foot to the other, widening.

Outside his window: the rains,
the quiet mornings. On the patio
a robin turning over twigs.

See how he eats, she says,
with a will to correct himself.

Neither she nor I know
how I could do such a thing,
but I give the chick away
to someone in the country.
She never looks at me the same again.
And I can't blame her, shod as I am
in these red fandango shoes,
wearing as I must
this gaudy dress, my unfairnesses
flashing like sequins.

Shopping

I would buy for my daughter earrings
of pale green and indigo glass.
She would think them funny,
would love them,
would say, What were you thinking?

In my mind I lay them into a carved
red box, the pads of my fingers
over the circles and petals on the lid.

Also this pair, the stones
red in the light, in the shade
black. I would be colorful and generous,

the fine lines in her throat, the shine
of her eyes. I buy a barrette
for the braid that sometimes lies above
the bones of her shoulders,
on the right or left when she turns.
A bauble, the light shining on it,
a yellow floating up inside the brown
under the surface. I want her hands
to open the clasp, her elbows in the air,
my daughter talking to someone when
she fastens it, or talking to no one
but herself in front of the mirror
in the morning. I want to have given,

to have wrapped in blue paper
crackling and wrinkling like
years of not going wild, of
sensible conservation.
She may think sometimes how I gave her
this or that, her hands opening.
She will wear it, this modest pin,
this abundant love, her rich dark hair.

Loving Her in the Mountains

Hard climb behind us,
we clown on the tundra,
my daughter and I,
laughing. The sleeves of my
too-big sweater swing limp
beyond my hands. She pushes

the bandana over my eyes.
I dance for her blindfolded, happy,
the water in the canteen
sloshing with my spinning and
twirling. My daughter laughs
until no sound comes and she
must sit, voiceless, on the rocks
to recover. On this day

in this place,
the peaks standing watch,
I love her
and I can only
dance it, my old shoes
quick as the feet of a deer
on the grasses.

I Tell Her of the Downy Gentian

I tell her of the prairie cemetery,
mowed twice every summer.
I tell her how, after fifty years,
the mowers died or moved away,
and the prairie, ungroomed,
grew noisy with grasshoppers,
hands of big bluestem
in the air all summer long.
The downy gentian,
fifty summers cut off at the throat,
bloomed that September

purple and strong:
bright cups set down in tallgrass prairie.
My daughter moves barefoot as if in fields
through the rooms of her house,
her body bending over books,
silhouetted in windows,
thin hands scraping carrots, slicing onions.

Can you see her, deciding?
Can you see her, down into darkness
like the bones of a very fine hand?
The undeniable roots,
reaching down, staying.

Looking for Luck

When she stands at the sink, my daughter opens
the blinds, watches the yard for the mallards
that sometimes come, tipping side to side,
up the rise to spend time under the spruce
beside her door,

the drake and the hen loafing under
low branches of her tree. Sometimes
she looks out to see the neighbor's cat,

Chintu, coming like a drop of water
on a windshield, zigzagging left to
the clump of lilacs, right to the garage.
Chintu stops, listens to nothing, paw
held in front like a fork, stalking.

My daughter goes out to the cat, saying its name,
sitting down in the grass
under the clothesline so Chintu can
make a circle around her body,
can brush like a hand against her,
around again for good measure, the cat

looking here and there in the yard
while circling. My daughter's hand
on its back, its tail drawn through
her fingers like a yellow scarf.
She begins to suspect
this is lucky: borrowed cat, unbidden
mallards. When she opens her door,

something runs like an animal between
her feet into the house, something not visible
stands like a totem in the white cups,
sits on her life as if on a dish,
solid and round-bellied
as one green apple.

Last Sunday

Last Sunday he showed my daughter
some home movies,
me, pregnant
walking in the ocean, and Goofy
tweaking my nose at
Disneyland.
        I remember:
I am wearing the red
dress my generous friend gave me.
I begin to see my own
on-again-off-again way.
I laugh, in my California

cateye sunglasses, into Goofy's
white glove. Her father took the film
and the projector and the screen to her place,
showed her mother walking
a corner of Pacific, showed a thread
of red dress
over a swell of belly,
a young woman laughing,
knee-deep
in foam and waves.

Naming

Marjorie, my father said.
My father, cleanshaven, just out of a
bath, putting on his khaki shirt, his khaki tie,
naming his baby in front of the mirror
in the bathroom, buttoning buttons,
looking for his glasses, his boots,
catching the bus to the base.

My son, two years old, climbing a ladder,
his head appearing over the edge of the roof,
a matter-of-fact child at two,
coming to help,
my father looking up from pounding nails,
his eyes surprised,
his fingers holding a nail,
hammer hanging in his hand,
seeing the baby at the edge of the eave,
talking to him, calm on the outside,

talking him steady,
keeping him from falling like a hammer.
The heft and plumb of my father's voice
keeping things where they should be.
The child at the top of the ladder
seeing things from a new point of view:
the joists, the colors of wood, the house
in the making. My father coming like a spider
over the rafters,
his feet in his old leather shoes

softly across the open spaces,
his dry cracked hand closing
on the boy's arm as on a handle.
My father's voice calling my name,

as if naming.
At the top of the ladder,
squatting like an acrobat on a wire
holding the boy's arm.

A child at a height in the quiet morning,
looking at what can be seen,
at things to come,
as if receiving names:
Common, jack, rafter, valley, hip.
Heel, bird's mouth, pitch, rise.
Facia board, rake, soffit.
Tab nail, sixteen,
eight-penny, ring-shank,
galvanized.
Ceiling joist,
ridgepole,
dormer,
peak.
Bearing wall,
truss,
claw,
shakes.
Two-by-sixes.
Two-by-eights.
Two-by-tens.

How is Paul?

How is your son, my friend asks. How is Paul?
I want to answer: he goes at the relentless pace
he uses to hike Mt. Chapin. I want to say:
if he asks you to go with him up Chapin,
he will wait for you, hold back so you can rest,
encourage you, tell you how great it is at the top.
You'll keep going. On the way down,
you will get caught in the rain, buckets of rain,

dangerous lightning, got to get below tree line fast;
you'll do it, following Paul on the rocks and
the roots and the trail. How is Paul? He loads
two tons of logs on a one-ton pickup with
old thin tires. He piles the logs higher than the sides.
He gets in, tells you where to meet him, because after
he unloads the logs, it would be nice to walk at dusk
on the old railroad bridge over the Platte. You agree
and he starts the Ford, he revs it, you watch him
chug up to the first light. People in newer vehicles,
that's everybody, will go around him. He will ease up
to the next light, the butts of the logs lined up

at the back of his neck, blunt missiles, ready to
pile through the glass in the event of any sudden stop,
in the event he ever gets up enough speed to matter,
Paul on Highway 44 south of Kearney near the Platte.
How is Paul? He unloads the logs at the campsite,
having called ahead to arrange to donate them. You,
meanwhile, take the wrong turn in your vehicle, you

wander a road with campers on both sides,
you cannot find the river.
You follow the road, make the big loop, lost.
There are lights in the rearview mirror, and you
think maybe it's Paul. The lights
blink three times. You pull over.
The vehicle behind you hiccups like an old Ford.
Paul has found you because he figured maybe

you'd come this way, and he wants to know:
Do you still want to go to the Platte. And you do.
Because what other place could you want to be.
How is Paul. The Platte at night
shines through the holes in the black shapes
of trees. You walk beside him on the path,
the Platte white in the dark, the thumbnail moon
an opening in clouds
like a child's painting. How is Paul.
He stands on the bridge in the dark,
trying to figure out if it's one owl
or two, and where exactly the owls may be
in the silhouettes of trees
along the shining smooth Platte.
You are leaning on the wooden rail of the bridge,
tapping with your fingernail. He's tapping, you're tapping
softly the rhythm of the owl's call. Paul's practicing the pitch:
Whoo oo oo. Who. Who.

Looking for Meteors

The meteor shower does not materialize
this year; it peaks twelve hours early
and on another continent, but we don't know that,
my son and his wife of one month,
the three of us on the dam
looking up in the dark, shivering, my neck
bent like a piece of cardboard, creased,
looking for meteors. We jump and point
at a couple of false alarms, airplane lights
and a possible satellite. Paul and Tara

lie down on the grass to look up,
wrap themselves deep into
the coat they share, and I high-
tail it to the path, walking,
not searching anymore, walking the dam
in the cold northern air of October,
Arcturus hanging like a pearl almost within reach
in her appointed place on the throat of the west.
Polaris soft and shy--though everything does

turn under her arm. On the water, a raft of geese
laugh from time to time like happy drunks,
the lake their own smooth moonless sky.
Long I walk toward Antares, that homefire burning,
walk until when I turn, the wind in my face,
the stars of Cassiopeia herself
begin to look like the arms and legs of lovers: warm,
bunched, cocooned, wrapped in their own
unstreaked coat.

Assateague Island, October

My son stands in the ocean,
his shoes slung over his shoulder,
looking east past that place where
in the shell-green water
the water swells,
past the place where the wave,
though it has no beginning,
begins.
                                    Every wave
against his ankles, calves, knees.
He has said the crash of the waves
is the planet breathing. Blow
after blow, my breath slows,
matching.

For that time I pulled your hair
in anger, I am sorry.
Let this wave heal it. For that time
when I made you, a little boy,
so carefully apologize
for what didn't matter. Let it
be carried up in a handful
of small white bubbles.

When I fussed over you.
When I couldn't stop
even though you hated fussing.
Let this wave wash that.
When I talked too much
in front of your friends.
Let this water and foam
take it. When you were six,
in the hospital, fighting the bars,
the rails, my arms,
to climb out of the bed.
Let this wave take that away.

When I was busy growing up
and you needed me. Let this
whole blue-green ocean
breathe it away.

Tomorrow we will go to the
Vietnam Memorial, you and I;
it will be raining. We will stand
with others in the rain
and I will cry for the pink rose on the ground
and for the old man holding a black and white umbrella.
I will cry and you,

who do not cry,
will lay your palm like a rose
on the shoulder of my damp coat.

Name after name, name after name
rolls in us
and through us
healing you, healing me.

PRACTICALLY ONE

In the Pacific

In the photograph: five men
in t-shirts and khaki pants
on New Guinea, the cook tent
behind them, and behind the tent
palm trees and sand. My father
clean as a shell in the row of men,
young hair, muscled arms.

He told me he watched a native
resting in the ocean,
and when the man came out and
walked up the beach,
my father asked him how to do it.
Let the water have you, the man instructed.
Let her rock you side to side.
Don't tell the ocean what to do.

My father swam out far enough to make
the palm trees very small on the beach,
the sky huge and unchecked.
He lay as if in a bed,
up and down with waves,
far from the rivers of home,
cornfields lying fallow,
a cottontail loping across furrows.
Moss and minnows,
pebbles and sand of the prairie river.
Bullheads in a hole near the bank
where the water runs cold.

My father in the Pacific,
mouth and nose out of the water,
rising and falling with waves,
waves washing over him in the long dusk,
the water taking his body in,
holding it.

He rocked in the Pacific until dark,
his ears tuned to the silence of ocean,
his eyes, when he opened them,
seeing new stars.

Letter from My Father

The letter did not pass unnoticed,
the postmaster remarking on it as he gave it
through the window into my mother's
young hands. Her strong legs and
brown shoes taking her down the steps

and up the street to read it. My father's
hand, the scrawl he was ashamed of,
a lanky love unwavering
in the wavering lines,
the bumps of the *m*'s and *n*'s,
semaphores of the *t*'s.
Long rectangular cuts of the censor

filled with an airiness my mother
read and reread, her hands over
the loneliness of the yellow paper,
the duty of the black ink. Square-
cornered proof that he, on his island,

breathed and slept and waked,
as she on hers.

Practically One

He would stay. There were the cardinals;
there were the wild turkeys in the fog, their rounded backs
on the hillside like black shrubs. It was good
to work, egg sandwiches at noon, a gallon of iced tea
in the summertime, locusts wheezing the long hours,

brown leaves lying over everything in the morning,
half-filling the metal pails, the wooden
storage boxes. That red star, Antares, blinking
nightly above the southern horizon

while he watered the garden with a hose,
song of water soaking into earth
practically one
with the sound of crickets in the dark.

On the Bridge, Spring Thaw

Margaret was, my mother says, all over
Robert in the back seat. It was disgusting,
she says, to want him that bad and in public.
A floe as big as a car goes under the bridge
and piles up on the jam. Margaret, who couldn't

hold herself back, is now 70, or is it 80,
in a brick house you can see from the road.
She's just returned, my mother says, from
treatments. Pieces of ice float
in the river, their backs up and down
like horses kicking the sides of the stall.
Caught in an eddy, a triangle rotates,
bumping its corners on the bank. I name it

in honor of a night in August in the 40's:
Margaret, I say to myself, *Go for it*.
The triangle spins, the water washing gray
over it. We do not see it break free
as long as we watch,
the sun warm on our faces.

The Dahlias My Mother Gave Me

The dahlias my mother gave me grew too tall
last year, big-limbed, falling over themselves.
This spring I broke them off as I walked by,
their hollow stems
open like small throats,
the first set of leaves hanging like hands
at the ends of a woman's arms
when she says
That's how *that* is.

Two times I lowered them
and tossed the tops into the can.

The hybrid rose, Mr. Lincoln,
isn't going to make it,
too hot, I forgot to water,
I chose not to, I didn't look,
I had things to do.

Let the tail, I said, go with the hide.

I see the dahlias have dispersed.
They are lying low, as she used to say,
not sticking their necks out.
Staying home and tending to business,
playing their cards close to the vest,
keeping their noses clean.

I drag the hose around, stand in front of them.
I water the roots for a long time

In for a penny, in for a pound

for a very long time.

Letter to My Daughter

You lifted him, sleeping, out of the crib,
wrapped him in a blanket. You were
crying, smiling, opening the door when
I came up the steps; you had your
movie camera on your other shoulder.
You gave me the child
and you said you wanted to film

the handing over. I couldn't believe it
there in your kitchen, that you would give
him to me, that it would be important
to you, the handing over. I thought you'd
leave him sleeping and greet me,
take me in quietly to look at him.
We'd stand in the room and talk in
whispers, my arm around you,
and maybe you'd peel back the blanket
and show me the thin stalks of his legs,

womb-bent. We'd stand in the room and
watch him sleep, maybe I'd touch the round
curve of his arm, but you must have
lifted him when you saw my car on the street,
must have wrapped him
as I pulled into the drive
to give him,
a gift partly out of its paper
so that quickly and exactly
it could be seen how good,
how perfectly good.

The Wind Picks Up

North of Mission, the wind picks up.
Tumbleweeds scuttle across the road
in fits and starts: crabs on a beach.
Near White River, a farmyard swept clean
of every small thing. On the clothesline,
a towel struggling like a catfish, the wind
blowing as if to ripple the ice on the pond.

I stay the night at the house of one of my aunts,
studying the rugs and flowers and soaps and glass
of her guileless rooms. I am her kin, her stock.
At the table we sit before bowls and plates of food
and she talks of Al, of his funeral tomorrow.
We hear the roars and pauses of the wind. We don't
want to sleep. She talks of other deaths, other men,
of her father who lined up the sisters in the kitchen

for spelldowns and arithmetic, who played the violin
for them, his barrel body leaning forward and back
into the notes of *Go to Dark Gethsemane,*
the sleeves of his shirt rolled to his elbows.
We talk about the bell tree and the swing tree,
barn and house, rich smell of bread
and kuchen, potatoes frying in cream. The roof

will cave in, she says, in the first good snowstorm.
The roof will open, it's the way of things,
the snow or the rain on the cookstove,
its copper reservoir and fancy handles, the house
where her grandmother held her all night
in front of the oven, old woman in a chair, wrapped
in a blanket with a child in the dark kitchen,
her feet on the open oven door,
the clock ticking, the wind
as it is now, an old voice in the ear. Tomorrow

at the funeral the living will sit in rows before the coffin,
love and resentment and history and unfinished business
flowing between and around us.
In our chins and cheekbones, in the eyes,
or carriage of shoulders, something familiar.
Arm in arm for a moment. For a moment an old farm
deep in oak leaves, the bell tree cut down,
the roof of the kitchen going in the next storm.

Tonight my aunt opens a closet of quilts,
spreads them layer on layer on the bed to show me
the reds and near-reds of the star quilt,
the new green of the Irish chain, the clear whites
and yellows of all the double wedding rings.

Under the cotton of the oldest quilt, I dream
a dream of a dark man, a sofa in front of a window.
He and I, his room, his books.
The skin of his hand, my hand.

Sound of wind wakes me. All night the wind,
a man locked out, throws himself
again and again at the door of the house.

He Rang the Bell

My father rang the bell Sundays, sat in the pew,
not singing, his hymnal open on his knees,
heard a thousand times that he was a wretch
and a worm, but he didn't tell me to stay
in the church he stuck to. At the kitchen table,
a strand of hair hanging over his forehead,
he said: A person has to do what they have to do.

The night he was coughing and trying to
talk, I said maybe he should rest.
I wish he would have kept talking.
When I stand mornings at the window
and look at the pines in my backyard,
two Austrians and one blank space
where I had the diseased tree cut down,
I wish I had let him keep coughing
and talking when he wanted to,
lying against the pillows,
his arms and hands out on the sheets.

Another time he asked *Will you get my shoes.*
I'm going home. Will you help me.
I wish I would have looked for his shoes.
We could have made it as far as the elevator.
I wish I would have found my keys and his shoes.
I wish we would have tried.

After pushing his IV cart in the halls of the hospital,
bumping along beside him with the bags,
my father wearing his cap because his hair was
falling out, after his buddy Curly came to ask him
to try to drink the stuff in the little condensed milk cans,
after his sisters drove all night to stand in the hall
and come into his room by twos to say
goodbye, after these things,

after standing at the bed with my mother
in a ring with my sisters,
holding his big blocklayer's hand,
listening to the sounds in his throat

as he was trying to break through,
hoping the next pause in the noise
would mean he was free of it,

after holding his hand that last Sunday
and watching the crow on the rocks of the roof
outside his window, the bird flapping its wings,
I holding his hand,
thinking sometimes how he had
scratched the back of his hands
when he had been more conscious--
he'd had that habit,
scratching one hand with the other,
as long as I'd known him--

after thinking of him milking a cow
in the middle of a pasture,
or laying blocks, a carpenter's pencil
stuck at a funny angle under the edge of his cap,
or driving the old black and white Chevy,
fast, to Jamison to get parts,

after the nurse brought a plastic bag into his room,
laid in my needlework, a yellow quilt I never finished,
the newspapers, the wool slippers
I had brought him from Wales,

after she handed the bag to me, saying
he was a very good man--
I knew she would say the same
to the daughter of the next one
and yet I was grateful to her for saying it--

after these things
I was empty and calm as a field of grass.
A window opening on the rocked
surface of a roof. A slab of sky
in a strange city. A crow, flapping.

I Broke My Mother's Dish

After I gathered the pieces,
I saw a fragment
lying like a small bright crystal
on the white enamel of her stove.
She tried to pick it up, pressing
with the end of her finger,
picking it up that way, tried to say
it wasn't glass, didn't want me
to blame myself, showing me love
sideways, which is her way. How

can I write about her, my ideas
set out obscenely, garbage
at the curb. She lied,
said none remained, don't worry,
pressed her finger into a piece of glass
to pick it up. *Glass*, I say; she says
Salt. I cannot stop looking
for the shine of a forgotten shard.

I Don't Want to Think about You

Go talk to your friends in the town.
Sit in the tavern and play cards.
Stop tipping the rabbit hutch,
the rabbits dropping out the door like
brown and white marbles.
You're getting your crowbar,
smashing the hollyhocks,

hitting the pink and yellow ears
of the flowers with the heavy
hook of your crowbar, beating
on the ground, beating the straw
bale to pieces, pounding it, beating
the pump in the yard, prying up
the old sidewalk under the cedars
in front of the house, you're going into the
shed, you're beating your old model T,

opening the doors and hitting the windows,
the seat, dust rising every time you bring
the crowbar down, you don't have to
wreck everything like this, I forgive you,
none of this is necessary, you're
beating the stucco off the house, it's
falling off the walls like pieces of crackers.
Pounding the cedars, pounding the trunks,
breaking the mason jars in the bushel baskets,
you're going down the cellar steps, I could
push the door shut with my little girl hands,
I could keep you down there. I could roll
the heavy two-wheel cart over and I could

push it onto the door of the cellar, leave it
and run away. You are breaking jars,
gallons of pickles and applesauce. You're
in the kitchen, smashing a loaf of bread
on the white enamel counter, the crowbar

over your head, you bring it down,
you are smashing the curved glass
of the china cabinet, smashing the wood
itself as if it would bend over in the middle
holding its old stomach,

you rip the bed with the crowbar,
beat the mattress and the blanket.
I run to the cage in the living room,
where the canary is; in the bedroom you are
banging the metal of the bed, beating
with the crowbar, noise, iron,
it will shiver hands and arms,
it must make old evil hands hurt,
they must be numb.

                 I carry the cage
into the yard, I run to the road,
the cage bumping against my ribs,
I stand in the road, the noise
an anvil hammered, hammered,
hammered.

I open the door but the canary is afraid,
does not fly. It is afraid of my hand,

small in the cage.
For a moment I hold it
crumpled like yellow paper.
I draw out my hand, a bird,
throw it, a fist,
uncaged, into the sky.

Pulling Up Beside My Husband at the Stoplight

We are going to the same place
but we take two cars. Sunday morning
and there's not much traffic
so I pull up beside him at the light.
The sun is shining on the road.
Here he is in his car

beside my car,
the curve of his shoulder
through the glass, his face
fresh from a shave, his hair
against the brown of his neck.
He turns and blows me a kiss.
I watch it float on by. I ask
for another. I think of him
coming into the dark bedroom

in the mornings,
the sound of his workboots
across the carpet,
the scent of his face
when he finds me in the covers,
pulls the blanket away and
kisses my eyebrow,
the corner of my mouth,
tells me the weather report
and the precise time of day.
I roll down the window,

whistle in my throat,
pull my glasses crooked on my face,
do my best baboon snorting,
pound the horn
as if it were bread dough.
There's only the lady in the white Taurus
but he is embarrassed, glad to see the green.
I'm stepping on the gas,
catching up, wondering
what I can do at 56th and Calvert.

I Hear You in the Morning

I hear you in the kitchen
fixing breakfast, teakettle hitting the burner, toast
clicking down, two bowls thumping the counter.
Through the wall I almost see you,
your torso in your work shirt,
doing your stretches,
the small sounds of your bones
giving. Pulling up your knees,
stepping in place fifty times,
warming up. You have followed me

to hard brown chairs of lecture halls,
along Haines Branch Creek
in search of the white-throated sparrow,
signing papers for a house,
following me following children
to airports. I have followed you
up boulder fields, a mountain trail

the only time you've left me.
You up above at the snow of the glacier,
opening your blue pack,
looking down on the trees and the valley,
I below with the marmots on a rock.
I've followed you from train stations
in the streets of European cities,
never able to give enough suitcases
to slow you down. With an old towel

I've followed you around the fenders and
chrome and glass of your Buicks and Dodges.
I've followed you from room to room
to keep talking about the thing we are
fighting about, mostly fighting about
how we must keep talking.
When I turn over in bed, you follow me

in the dark of your sleep, folding me up
as if you would follow me to Minnesota,
to Michigan, to the sea, to the edge of
fifty years, breathing in, breathing out.
Above my head in the dark,
the crash of your breathing,
leading on.

I Lie About My Life

I was born in a house in town,
a house with a porch, a swing.
I cut my teeth on arrowroot cookies
and my face was hardly ever dirty.
It was a good school and my father wore a tie.
My mother made triangular sandwiches
or watched them made,
whichever is better. To save my siblings
embarrassment, I was an only child. I knew
sports and music. I was not so holy as to be
unfashionable. College, yes, but not too
seriously, as befits good breeding.
What am I saying?

I believed everything I read and after I had
laid my son into his crib for the night,
I studied at the kitchen table of my
basement apartment like a woman who
grew up in a small town,
sitting on the front step on main street in the morning,
the front step of a concrete block cafe,
alone before breakfast,
long before the first pickup
would roll into town from the south.
The sun rising, pinking the gray
behind the White Horse Bar
and the cream station.
The sparrows making their unsophisticated
noise in their messy nests
under the eaves of the post office.
The only two-story building,
the only child, the only human being.
Barefoot, surveying the gravel of main street.

Getting Well in the Mountains

In the mountains my daughter
wanted to play cards. The four of us
played pitch quietly, her baby sleeping in the next room.
We had to guffaw quietly and say *damn* quietly
and pound the table quietly. She bid cautiously
and cared too much and she thought with her brother
as her partner they would whip us bad, but

I played so loose I couldn't lose, bid on nothing
and got the ace in the blind. I went set
more than anybody and yet we won.
I hardly knew the score most of the time. I bid 7 or 8.
You can always make 7; all you have to do is
bid it first before anybody else. The games were hilarious
because she is witty and Paul is fun
and Don began to take some risks. Remember how Heidi

got well in the mountains, ate bread and cheese and ran
rosy-cheeked through the alpine asters,
slept in the loft of her grandfather's hut at 10,000 feet,
played with the goats and the goatherd
and got healthy in every way. My daughter
got stronger and stronger.
She had her own cabin, slept long
and walked down in the morning,
her boots crunching the gravel. I'd see her coming

and tell the baby and turn him loose
to run out and greet her. She'd come in for pancakes,
sit down, and ask how he slept last night. Sometimes
she'd go to town, play miniature golf and go to movies,
or hike up to lakes. Don took her to the Stanley for lunch
and Paul built her a fire under the stars

and toasted marshmallows for her. After the first night
I thought maybe she wouldn't want more pitch
because it's boring to play with somebody who
bids all the time but no, the next night

she wanted to know if we'd play cards again.
I want her to enjoy the lake and the child and all her life
all her life.

I'm trying not to worry because
worry is stupid. Action is the thing.
I want to listen because when I listen
I learn that what she really wants is
to move the crib into my cabin and what she really wants is
to carry the baby on her back down the trail. We stood
on the bridge and watched the water wash the rocks,
watched two streams come together, tried to remember
which is Wind River and which is Glacier Creek.
The peaks we know better and we name them together: Otis,
Hallets, Thatchtop. Longs. Mount Lady Washington.
Storm. Teddy's Teeth. What she wants is to go ahead
in the hot sun into the valley or up to Ouzel Falls. I stay
in the shade with the child. I want to give her time

and space and a hug every morning. I want to say
your hair looks so good and that's a great shirt.
What I want is the window open,
the best air in the world coming in, the lake very blue,
the undersides of the trees very green.
What I want is to tell her:
Pretend you have the Ace King Joker.
What I want is to say:
Bid high. Name trump.

Taking the Baby to the Marsh

We walk the wetland,
our weight lowering the pontoon boardwalk,
my daughter carrying her son, telling him

about the marshgrass, telling him where he is.
He is in her arms; she is wrapping the blue blanket
around him, pulling his cap to cover his ear.
I want to remember how she holds her son,

turns him to see the Canada goose walking,
the goose laying his flat hands down again and again
on the boards. Now the baby watches,
his face all interest for the take-off,

the honking, the wings grazing air.
It is my turn; I take the child,
pull the wings of my coat around him.
As he is falling asleep I whisper

into his soft new ear. I say: *red twig, black water.*
I say *king goose, queen hawk.*
I say *grass.*
I say *wind.*
I say *mother.*

She Asks for Baby Pictures

She asks for baby pictures to see if
her son resembles her.
I don't have many.
Welcome to the world, my
daughter's son. It's lousy,
but there are mountains, rows of them
for the eye on a warm morning in summer.
They have snow and names and trails.
Welcome to the world. My grandmother

had no fancy way to cut apples, no stars showing
in the center; she halved the plain
yellow apples after she picked them
off the ground. She fingered the fruit
in her palm, cut it. This is the harvest
given for you: the sun, the wind

clapping the branches together,
the storm, the morning after.
The air full of bees, the tractor
parked in the grove. The basket
full of apples, the pail full.
This apple, this Macintosh, this knife,
this old loose skin, finger and thumb
picking out the brown hard tear

of the seed. This is your stock;
you are one of us, plain cut,
nourishing, no photographs, you
must remember it or throw it away.
Peel it, don't peel it, bake it in a glass
dish, a few raisins in the bubbling
juice, or lay it in a pie shell, spread
out, buttered, sugared, covered over,
browned. A freckle-face pie crust. This

is what you are: a variety that lasts
the winter, doesn't run out, slice
after slice falling into the dish. No
recipe, no pedigree, no fooling.
This: leaves withering when it is time,
fruit holding onto a solid shape, an honest color,
applebutter in the jar. Macintosh, Jonathan,
Yellow Delicious, Northern Spy.
The crack of the knife.

IN THE RAIN

Resurrection

After the spring snowstorm
I go out to save trees, shaking them
as if they were sleepers,
hanging on when they lift,
standing in waterfalls of snow,
my hair awash with it,
my earrings cold on my neck.

I crack off a dead limb from the redbud
and use it, a scepter,
on the forsythia: yellow flowers
bloom out of snow. The yews
rise, healed. I get carried away and
go on to someone else's woods to save trees.

I reach into snow, feeling for femur,
for tibia, ulna, radius,
pulling them up, shaking them,
hitting them with my pole,
my face up to snow coming
down, my mouth open to eat,
glasses covered, snow behind the lenses,
wet snatches burning my cheeks where
I brushed against cedars.

I turn back toward the house,
an old man stumbling,
my jacket whitened,
arms hanging as if long branches,
hands numb in my gloves,

a grin on my blind face.
I walk through drifts chanting:

Rise.

Rise.

When I Sliced through the Nail

When I sliced through the nail
and into the barrel of the finger,
I wrapped my hand in a dishtowel,
walked out of the kitchen, not telling
anyone, paced in the dark up and down
the sidewalk in front of my house, sometimes
holding my hand aloft, for the pain,
as if feeding gulls. Under a popsicle
stick and gauze it healed so well it

amazed me. Then, talking,
I'd sweep that fingertip along my chin,
the small places of my skin
looming large as bumps on a basketball;
my old wound, before it got used to things,
magnifying the terrain.

White Semi

I get down on my hands and knees on the asphalt
at the truckstop to scooch way down into what
in yoga we call the child position, and I turn
my head and look and look under the semi of my life.
I go to the front of the cab, I kneel down again on
a mostly greaseless spot and I gawk under,

pretending to know Peterbilt and Kenworth.
The guys inside the truckstop and the guys
at the gas pump are watching. They know I know
nothing. They know this white semi is not a semi at all;
it is a yellow Yugo or a green Geo Metro or an orange
Escort or a blue Neon and I am looking under it
because I am pretending to be able to assess any damage

I might have done and whether it is safe to drive. I know
they will laugh, make a crack about my highly developed
stupidity and the highly developed stupidity of people
similar to me who cower in the child position on their knees

looking for they know not what on the underbelly
of their low-slung lives. The guys at the pump
and the candy machine know vehicles and they know
life and they know that I do not, because they saw me
run my vehicle up over a curb, more than a curb, an

expanse of concrete embankment because I was in
the wrong lane, the wrong side of the highway.
I was there, I don't know how I got there, and traffic
was coming, and I had to get my miserable life
up out of the wrong lane temporarily
and find a spot of concrete to crawl out upon and
look up into the wires and pipes, dirty mysterious
bolts and plugs, nobody to help me--I don't give a

diddlysquat--I am a nimrod and this is my four-wheeled
no-warranty life, all of it, axle and oil pan,
drive shaft and differential. This is my life, this is my
work, this is my bygod perspective and I am going
to get back in and slam the door--No, I am going to
jam on my leather helmet, stick out my tongue,
adjust my goggles and my long purple scarf,
straddle my new red Harley Davidson Ultimate
Chopper and roar-- do you hear-- ROAR away.

Asking

I did not ask about the foxhole
in New Guinea, about the
dogs, the black one with curly hair.
I did not say Tell me the first thing
you can remember.
What was it like, winter on the farm,
moonless mornings. Who taught you
the trumpet and did you like to dance.
How did they tell you *cancer,* how

did they say it, did you know before
the word. Did you leave home.
What was your father like, what did
he call you. Will you hate it
when I write about you. After your dying,
one more quiet thing you did well,

I stand in the wind in the cemetery
with my daughter and my son,
a small ring of arms and shoulders
on that huge flat grass you have begun
to be under. *Let the dance begin,* I say.
I say, *Can we?*
and they close in
as if one hand
taking another, as if asking,
as if giving, permission.

It's Been Written

The whole world has happened before.
It's been written in cucumber vines, tendrils
reaching out slower than the eye can follow.
It's repeating itself in a saxophone
or a pipe organ, someone reaching

with her foot to a low note,
her hands moving on keyboards.
Diapason, flute, reed, it's been
written. My father's face
has been written, wishing me well,
even when I'm against myself.
My daughter's been written and
her daughter not yet born. My son
on Deer Mountain writing a letter,
the wind ruffling his hair and the pages.
Air passing over a crow's wing,
over the fissures in each
black feather, not quite
soundless: that's been written.
Bullsnake swimming in the Platte,

raccoon hit by a car at dawn
on Eldon Drive, lying on his side
like a gray plush toy, his ear
flared toward the sound
that would hit him. Pine cones a foot long
from a tree growing a thousand years; the man
who wants to cut it down, to put his
saw into the tree at the height
he can reach. My child's voice
on the phone saying Love you
or Have a good time
or It was a rotten week.
That's been written. I'm writing it
all again, words once again
one after another,

as a pebble puts down its rings,
as many as it can
on its way to the bottom,
rings showing the shape the stone had,
the only shape it can make,
this one time,
like all the rest,
rings inside rings,
rolling swiftly out and away
from that place in the lake
where the stone slips under the skin.

Becoming My Father

My father is dead so it falls to me
to say it myself. I say: *Isn't that
quite something?*
The ears of the deer move

but her eyes stay on me.
We face one another, the deer and I,
in the road in the morning by the river,

her hooves perfect sculptures on gravel, her legs
very young maples, curved and sinewed,
her nose wet-black,
neck so alert and living I wish I could

hold her. She moves off
lightfooted as birdsong, as wind
through a single cottonwood.

Looking back before she jumps the fence
she says nothing

as he would say it.

Wind Tore at Her House

Wind tore at my grandmother's stucco
house, at the screendoor she held open.

Wind whipped her hair, tearing at her words,
at her flowered apron snapping like a flag.

Today I looked at my hands
slicing tomatoes

or going along on the page,
my pen nodding up and down

in my grandmother's hand

her old loose skin, my
old loose skin. I reject her:

round poor heavy-footed.
I take her for my own:

my own faint trail, two tire tracks
in the grass across the land.

Grandmother, like a wind,
have me, hair and all. Come,

wind, old grandmother,
come.

Why We Last

Perhaps my thumbs, over and over,
hard against the bottom of your feet,
my thumbs into the pad of each toe,
along the arch, the unyielding heel,
I sitting on the floor, you
lying crosswise under the covers,
one foot at a time hanging out
over the side of the bed. Perhaps
the fights, my crying face,

my mad face, yours. The one time
I thought you were going to hit me
because I wouldn't quit talking,
pushing. That one time I thought
you were going to strike.
And how the surprise made me half-
laugh, and then my laugh
surprised me, and of course you
didn't but the power was there,
there in your back. Your back
bare, bending over me.
In a yellow shirt, bending over
your shoes to tie them.
Your workboots set

one beside the other
in the left side of the closet,
always the laces placed inside,
and the ring of keys. Perhaps
how you don't want to talk,
you just want me here in the house,
snow filling the yard,
a woodpecker hanging onto the suet,
his black so stark, his red
so clean. My white arms waking
in the predawn, pushing open
the sheets, pulling you in.

Perfume Counter, Dillards

She shows him cologne, thinking
that's what he means, a thirty-dollar
plastic spray bottle. No, he says,
his check book open flat on the glass
of the counter. No, in his bargain
t-shirt, fifteen-dollar haircut,
Wards jeans. No, he says
softly, Perfume. She brings up

from the depths in their white boxes
one-quarter ounce,
one-third ounce,
one-half ounce, and
tells him the price of each,
which he sort of knows from
last time. And I in my five-year old
Lake Superior many-washed gray

sweatshirt and my hair all over
the place with rain and wind and
the wrong shampoo know
what she doesn't:
he'll take the real thing, the big size
and because I further know if I should be so
foolish as to give up the ghost,
kick the bucket, cash in my chips,
he would--not that he's fickle-- eventually buy
some good brand for some other woman,

I make my plan--
the universe being thrown together as it is--to live,
to be the no-substitute,
the real,
the one hanging in there
beside him while he writes the check
and signs it and draws a line
under his name.

Saying Yes on the Road

My husband and I are singing in the car,
passing a red pickup from Indiana which
looks like every pickup we have ever passed.
In the old days when our song came up on the tapes,
the kids in the back were embarrassed,
my husband holding my hand
and singing toward the white lines
in the highway, asking me not to

leave him lonely.
It's a new song today,
our songs like our hands having changed,
softer, not so needy, not so sleek.

By day the lush green corn or dry brown stalks.
At night the bridges and the flat white rivers under the moon,
the lights of cities flung on the dark.

My husband in the front, driving, singing.
And I, in the back, my papers and books
spread around me.

He's reaching over his shoulder to touch my hand,
my hand reaching up to him,
as if the concave of our palms
could get closer to this closeness,
as if we could give *yes* to what comes beyond the rise,
beyond this swell of ground the road follows.

Afraid to Be Old

Afraid to be old, to have someone paid
to place food into your mouth, your daughter coming
daily, when she is in town, to strap
on the wrist brace, fit your glasses to your face,
inquire about the hearing aid. The choice
you will have is to spit or not to spit
but your haircut and your walk and your books

will be gone, the purée
holding to your chin and your bib.
You don't want to soil the sheets,
will rise out of the haze almost awake,
try to call in the manner of someone
in a dream who must shout.
The others in the room will know
you want something, you are half raised up,
your eyes closed, reaching, and of course
the relatives in a circle will

do the proper thing, the wrong thing,
try to calm you and cover you.
You are trying to make it to the bathroom
one last time but you can't
and you lapse into the bed;
the nurse will be kind when
she cleans you. She will ask
the others to leave the room.
Though your eyes are closed,
she will talk to you, calling you by your
given name. *It's all right,* she will say.
It's all right.

Why Do You Remember Your Father's Suit

Why do you remember your father's suit,
blue, thin, the same every Sunday,
winter and summer, no overcoat,
weekdays a hooded sweatshirt to keep the back
of his neck warm, the weathered skin between
the curve of his back and the incline
of his head, collared on Sundays,
the dark suit on his shoulders,
his Saturday night kitchen haircut above it,
why write about him, why not love
your father some other way, let him

alone, let him drive his pickup,
pulling the flatbed up the long hill,
too slow, too slow, going to
lose it. Open the door, he said. Jump
if we jack-knife. Why write his words,
the gravel road, the door open,
the engine growling, not going
to make it, you yourself ready to
jump and roll, the river behind you,
the road, the bridge, a line of trees, your father
looking at the road and the rear view mirror
and the dials on the dash, he is dead

and you are inventing him, claiming
his blessing as you make him up,
why write about that suit, about
the nape warm, unchilled, why bend him
over his tractor in November, a wrench in
his ungloved hand, why not leave him,

banging metal, leave the clanging of it,
a bright cold bell under the hackberry trees,
you are ready, you will jump if necessary,
leave him reading his Reader's Digest in the
morning in the quiet house, let him carry

a log, let him lay it on the embers, let it
smoke, let it burn, let him drive fast
on the dirt road, the dust rising behind him,
fast into South Dakota to catch you in
your friend's car, north on your way
toward college without your suitcase,
let him catch you on the highway, pull up
beside you, flag you down, let him place

what you need into the trunk of the car,
let him close it, his bare hands on the lid,
the wind around his shoulders, around his
face, let him say, again, Goodbye.
Be good.

The Last Thing He Said

The last thing he said was
Yes. Maybe he was answering my mother's
question, maybe it was mine. I wanted
to be sure he had enough morphine, enough
of anything he wanted. It had shrunk
to one room. One breath at a time
pulled like knotted twine
in and out through a hole in a board.
Louie can you hear

The morning his watch wouldn't fit,
my mother said something was wrong
with the clasp. She laid the watch
back on the table. *Swollen*, he said, *swollen too damn big
for the watchband.* A spade, he maintained,
is a spade.

Sometimes I rise and roam the house
a woman with fears
window to window
Louie can you hear me
Are you in pain

For no good reason--
parallelograms of moonshine
on the cool dark floors--
I am beginning to feel safe:
a woman with fears
a woman with love

frost on shingles
oak trees
grass.

The World Was Not Enough

bearing down, pressing me out into
the world that was not enough for her without me in it
                                                --Sharon Olds

It was Sunday morning, and when I got home
from the prairie, my son had gone to church, so
I put on my jacket and went too. When I entered
the building, I waited to see if I'd get a feel
for which side to go to, which side he was on,
but two women talking loud in the anteroom
ruined my concentration. I went to the
south side and tried to see through the watery glass
in the door, crouching to see if anyone
sat in the blur I thought was the back of a chair.
I opened the door a crack, no usher to stop me
because the service was two-thirds over,
and I saw him

across the room on the other side--
blond, big, intense--how I love that
unplanned child, love his happiness
and unhappiness, his generous grin and
the sort of sideways hop he will do, coming to give
me a hug when he sees me in the kitchen in the morning or
when he comes home happy. I saw him, arms crossed,
glasses, saw all in one second, saw the heaviness
of the tweed coat on the warm day,
his face turned to the speaker,
one inch and one second all I needed, but I
looked at him long and enjoyed it, and went

around through the room where
the women were still talking. I went to
the clouded glass of the double doors on that side,
had to look through the crack again.
I sat in the last row with the ushers and
watched the hair on the back of my son's
head and thought about the world,
the world that is not enough for me without him in it.

Saving the Photograph

Above my desk I pin the photograph I should
throw away, the one that didn't turn out:

shape of my son against the window,
his face and shirt uninterrupted black,
light catching the edge of his glasses,
placing at the corner of his unseen eye
a small bright moon.

Behind his silhouette,
sunlight in the yard,
the Kentucky coffeetree caught in mid-sway
as if my father, a young man,

came in out of the light,
argument a mere shim

his arms crossed,
cap, ears,
restitution, second chances

hardly more than arm's reach.

My Son Cooks

My son cooks a meal for me on Mother's Day,
searching on his knees
for the saucepans and skillets,
chopping his way through peppers and onion,
smacking the garlic with the flat
of the knife, peeling papers from the clove
in his unhurried way. The menu in his handwriting,

the soup, the eggplant, the rice he's sure I'll like.
Cook's helper, I wash the bowls and forks
when he lays them down.
Doing two things at once he says when
he over-browns a slice or two.
Just right when the sauce fills to the top of the dish.
Opening the oven, wiping his hands on his apron,
he sings:

> *I'm looking through you,*
> *where did you go?*

I shake out the green tablecloth he brought from Guatemala,
lay the plates: an English scene in browns and a bit of red,
the colors right but the snow and the trees far from El Salvador
where he called me on the day the sons
wear flowers for their mothers,
red if she's living, white if she's dead.
I'm wearing red for you, he said when he
finally got through on the phone. *I'm*
glad it's red. It was a call I nearly missed,

the phone ringing in the middle of the night,
the operator a small voice in my ear. *Ball.*
Ball. Ball-o. I hung up,
told my husband it's nobody. Then I sat
upright. Please call back, please try again.
How could I be this stupid. Idiot, dolt.
Wrapped in a blanket, I went to another room,
stared at a phone until it rang. Yes, yes, I told
the warbling. Yes. Paul. Paul. Paulo.

I pull on my boots and go to the lilacs, scissors
in hand. When the vase is full, I add one columbine in the middle.
Through the meal it holds itself
above everything. In the morning I find
leaning against the vase
a picture he took of himself a few days ago
in front of the lilacs. Surrounded by purple,
he's wearing red.

When She Calls

When my daughter calls
I listen for the legacy I gave,
passed to her as it was passed to me,
worn shiny as an old silver spoon:
fear
panic
my grandmother standing
in the photo of the farmyard,
a woman feeding chickens, having

thrown grain on the ground,
now looking into the eye behind
the camera. Passing it on.
The word she used was *hopeless*.
She said she didn't want to live

blindsided by blackness
on any given morning
but she did--
and passed it on
and with it a round-shouldered
strength, feet firmly
on the ground, hands empty but
undefeated,
going about the afternoon
as it is, not changing anything for show,
not even standing up straighter for the lens,

just there, just summer, just hard times,
turning back to the house or the barn,
to the field or the table,
keeping on
keeping on.

In the Rain

They'd been downtown and when
they got near home, my daughter asked her husband
to let her off at Michael's. He drove on home
with the baby and she had Michael cut her hair.
Michael exclaimed over it, said it was healthy and gorgeous,
and though he says such things,
the fact remains: the curtain

of it, the curve leaning toward her throat.
Michael said things she needed to hear
from a stranger, someone who should know,
said that he would blow it dry
and curl it a little. She didn't prefer that
but it was OK, she would have him do it
if he wanted to. She stepped out

of the shop, hoping he'd think
she was going only to her car,
that the curl he'd ironed into the ends
would last the evening
but she knew in the rain it would
take its own shape again.
She walked along Dale Street,
turned up Moundsview, her hood
slipping down on Kent,

thunder or her laughter, or both, on Ryan,
her husband and the baby waiting,
headlights and puddles on Roselawn,
the trees holding their budding fingers
out for rain, her face up,
her coat open on Rice Street,
jumping the last sunken snow
as if over a bed of tulips,
dancing along South McCarrons
toward home, ruining her hair,
making it beautiful.

My Old Aunts Play Canasta in a Snowstorm

While there is time I must read the wrinkles
under each faded blue eye, related to my
father's blue eye, related to me. I must ride along
in the backseat; the aunt who can drive will

pick up each sister at her door, six in all, will keep the Pontiac
chugging in each driveway while one or the other
puts her overshoes on and steps out, pulling
the door shut with a click, the wind

lifting the brown fringe of her white cotton scarf
as she comes down the sidewalk, still pulling on her
new polyester Christmas-stocking mittens,
right hand, left hand. We have no business to be
out in such a storm, she says, no business at all.

But the wind takes her laughing cracking voice
and lifts it and she sinks into the backseat or
the frontseat. On to the next house, the next
sidewalk, the heater blowing to beat the band.

It is a good canasta day, the deuces wild
even as they were in childhood, the wind
blowing through the empty apple trees, through
the shadows of bumper crops. The cards line up

under the long finger bones; eights and nines and aces
straggle and fall into place: long-time habits, or well-
behaved children. My aunts
shuffle and meld, the discard pile frozen,
the wind a red trey to be remarked upon, remembered,

and appreciated, because, as one or the other says,
We are getting up there in the years; we'll
have to quit sometime. But today,
today,
deal, sister, deal.

Keeping My Mother Warm

I gave a down shirt: rib-knit collar, snaps,
forest green. She said she wears it in the house.
I gave a jacket: royal blue, zipper, hood, premier
northern goose down. When she scrubbed

makeup off the collar, she bleached
the color out but she said she doesn't mind.
I gave a black cotton sweater, a jillion red roses
embroidered on the front, heavy as chain mail,

elastic in the cuffs. She said she washed it,
dried it in the dryer, said it held up
pretty well. I gave a sleek wool blend, gray
with white cables. Perhaps it flaps

on her washline even now. Maybe it tumbles today,
cuffs over crewneck, in her dryer.
I should make her a quilt. A quilt
for the quiltmaker. Last night I slept

under a quilt she sewed: gorgeous prairie,
sea of many colors. Red velvet triangles,
yellow satin trapezoids, purple silk
parallelograms, dark shining rhombuses--

her feather stitch holding every crazy thing
together. Thanks, Mom, for that beauty.
May your loneliness go south for the winter.
May your old friends bring you cake. May you

beat them at pitch, pinochle, hearts, and gossip.
May the mail arrive early with gifts. May
hummingbirds remember where all your
windows are. May your feet be warm as

waffles, warm as buckwheat cakes, warm as
sweethearts. May your fingers limber and
bend above any patch you ever want. May all your
pies be chocolate. Love, Me. Love me. Love me. Love me.

Storm at Night

About one in the morning on Indian Island
the wind wakes me, sucking in the sides of the tent.
The lightning so bright that after it is gone,
it remains on the back of my eyelids.
On the back of my eyelids the hoops and zippers
of the inside of the tent. Thunder
close and huge over me. The rain beating on the tent,
on the purple poppy mallow, as I imagine it,
low against the ground in the dark.
Talons of the screech owl
grasping the substance of the tree.

When things settle down to rain,
the surface of the Platte, as I imagine it,
peppered as if with stones,
I am thinking of my friend who,
when he knew he was going to die,
sat in his yard in the sunshine
with his neighbor. The two of them
on blue lawn chairs drinking Stroh's.
Rolling cigarettes, making a trough with
the index finger in squares of white paper,
shaking the tobacco into the trough, rolling,
licking the papers, trying again.
Both of them not smokers, smoking.
Not talking about illness.

The Platte flowing from its source
around and over gray boulders, flowing
beside Indian Island, beneath thunder,
white for a moment under lightning,
its broad surface wrinkling like skin.
I am thinking of Crazy Horse, who
before he died, asked for the man who had
pushed the bayonet into the soft parts of his back.
Asked for that one to stand before him, and spoke
to him of pardon. Crazy Horse lying
in his bloody graveclothes.
His mother and father receiving the
body of their light-haired child
to put into the cart.

After rain, not sleeping, thinking.
A wind high in the cottonwoods,
the crickets stroking the dark.
Thinking of my daughter who called
to say she cut her hand with a
knife in her kitchen. My daughter
far down the flow of the Platte,
learning my grandmother's remedy,
using her poultice of sugar and
alcohol. The cut, as I imagine it,
healing. My daughter, her smooth
brown hair, as I imagine it, hanging

above their hands. Young woman's
hands, old woman's hands
laying the white poultice against
the red line of the scab,
winding strips of cloth,
wrapping the wound.
The Platte from its source
peppered by night rains.
In the morning the water sparkling
like leaves turning in wind.
The Platte wrinkling over its sand bars,
around the smooth white bones
of its cottonwood logs.

Having this Afternoon Turned Away

Having this afternoon turned away her only visitor--
a persistent swallow trying to build a nest
under the eaves--my mother expects no one.
Another evening with the lamp and the TV, my father

long dead, his smile, his hair.
Her nephew Eddie

driving from South Carolina
stops by, detouring to see her,
surprise her if she's home. Mischief
in his eyes, he raps on the door, his hair

a rascal yellow.
My mother at the table, the remains
of her supper on a single plate, sees

in the dusk what she looks for,
out of distance, out of the least
possible light,

my father's blonde head,
his shoulders, his stance at her front door,
reflected or real,

the long embrace of the stranger,
arms closing in a wingbeat
to gather the irreplaceable
safely home.

As If I Were Looking at Photographs

As if I were looking at photographs,
I see my son backlit before a window,
everything that can be inferred,
including his crossed arms,
my father's.

My daughter dances on Mount Chapin,
her feet quick on the rocks,
her hands lifting the crepe paper of her arms,
or she sits in a backyard I must
get used to calling hers,
in her arms the neighbor's cat,
my daughter's hair moving over
her shoulders as she aims
the cat at the lens.

An old sepia--so much to learn--
I hold a cloth doll, my white stockings
wrinkling at the knees, my hair a curl lopping
over, fuzzing out.

After an argument,
as if waiting for the sound of a shutter,
my husband pauses, hands
hanging on the hooks of his wrists;
his face quizzical.

My daughter hangs the clothes,
the cat in the grass drawing
one hip and then the other,
soft finger of tail,
over her ankles. My son,
looking more and more
himself, moves out of shadow.

Meanwhile my husband, choosing once more
to cross a distance,
places his hands on my shoulders,
says something forgiving into my hair.

Today

Today on the anniversary of my father's death
I walked on the dam among the geese,
the whole flock quiet as they are sometimes
when you walk through them at sunrise,
then one shaking out her wings
and running toward a direction,
the others in the air with her

before you can figure out who is truly the leader.
It was twelve years ago today, giving as little trouble
as he could, dying on a Sunday
in the daytime, not thrashing about.
The geese lift off, folding their legs back as if
that's the way they prefer it,

slipping into air, their toes pointed behind them.
He had smiled in photographs,
happy to stand beside his beloved,
the space ready, the year of birth

cut into granite, numbers already there,
curves in speckled polished stone.
Today there are old songs on the radio
and we sing along together in the car,
my husband and I, two fools
singing down 27th Street, weaving in and out,
sitting in the line backed up at the light,

singing If I Had a Hammer,
singing Puff the Magic Dragon,
singing Old Stewball Was a Racehorse,
singing That's What You Get for Loving Me:

> *I ain't the love you thought I'd be*
> *I got a hundred more like you, so don't be blue*
> *I'll have a thousand 'fore I'm through*

and we don't care
if we look ridiculous, singing
and jabbing each other. The light's green
and there's another song coming.

Marjorie Saiser was born in El Paso, Texas, and grew up in north central Nebraska, near the Niobrara and the Keya Paha. In 1980, she received a Master's Degree in Creative Writing from the University of Nebraska-Lincoln, winning the Vreelands Award and the Academy of American Poets competition.

Her poems have appeared in *Prairie Schooner, Georgia Review, Cream City Review, Laurel Review, Zone 3, Crazy Horse*, and numerous other journals. Her work has been anthologized in *Adjoining Rooms* (Platte Valley Press, 1985), *Wellsprings* (University of Nebraska-Kearney, 1995), *Leaning into the Wind*, (Houghton-Mifflin, 1997), and in *The PlainSense of Things* (Sandhills Press, 1998). She has been a finalist for the Intro Award (Four Way Books), the Robert Penn Warren Prize, the New Letters Literary Award, and the Billy Murray Denny competition. She is currently the author member of the Nebraska Literary Heritage Association and a speaker for the Nebraska Humanities Council .

She lives in Lincoln, Nebraska, with her husband Don. They have two children and one grandchild. Her favorite thing to do is to get the whole family together for a walk on Nine-Mile Prairie.